I0829968

8THE FEB 2020
FACEBOOK TWITTER AND INSTAGRAM ACCOUNTS HACKED
BBC NEWS

LEE WAITE

authorHOUSE

AuthorHouse™ UK
1663 Liberty Drive
Bloomington, IN 47403 USA
www.authorhouse.co.uk
Phone: UK TFN: 0800 0148641 (Toll Free inside the UK)
        UK Local: 02036 956322 (+44 20
        3695 6322 from outside the UK)

Published by AuthorHouse 08/07/2020

ISBN: 978-1-7283-5583-2 (sc)
ISBN: 978-1-7283-5584-9 (e)

Print information available on the last page.

This book is printed on acid-free paper.

Dear sir /madam Or manager

We been having same problem. This where ours started having problems our Facebook:

We been hacked our using my name on Facebook. First girl accused lee name as EMMA

Spreading news on the social media Facebook. Saying that lee cheating on u Sandra. I WAS GOING REALY MAD when I herd about this. This kept on so many years we both been rowing lot

PHONE CALLS

Even been coming in two sandra phone
to. This having been about 4 years
problems. Over just 1 girl. Sandra said
two me lee are u seeing emma. Said no
only time saw Emma out. When all boys
out then been spreading.

ROOMERS ABOUT me

Like having phone calls coming two my mobile at 8:o'clock morning time:

Living address at time Bethlehem road skewen. I put my self underrest stop me going two pub and take any kind of weapon cause do shot kan karate coming two my black belt.

Was only in side for 1 nite only. Not even police do any thing about it two about Facebook problem law dont care these days. Said two sandra let's go back two church. That's what we done I did not have any clue that people could hack in or pretend two be me. Only thing been doing putting mobile phone number in 4 pass word to change pass words. Been doing that for very long time:

One of our family members in church put our Facebook secure u are lee sandra facebook secure done said thank u. Thought it was done person. Pretending two be me came back on seen Facebook. All restarted again. What could I do about this nothing or police wood not do anything rowing still kept on. We christan people. Goes two mount pleasant. Baptist church swansea king way

I decided two say two sandra let's move some where else sandra said ok leston to me I said yes. Moved up road two bedroom cottage we took it on been living ear since. Sandra looking for her cousin Jenny two while we still having problems face book. Lee been accused one after another.

Sleeping with women on Facebook I bought a bran new pc computer from pc curry pc world what I decided two do then is two join up control pc with pc team know how £70 per year pc problems technology services two be safe on pc.

We both got married in our church on my 50th birthday same day. Sandra cousin named jenny came two our wedding we been having problems Facebook long time wedding went realy good.

We paid for DJ all day for wedding also bus laid on for sandra friends come two wedding had photos done laid good food on eving. Be for we got married I was accused seeing Jenny two words been put in photos of jenny and friend together put in saying words about me

pretending two be Jenny on face book. Saying that I'm sleeping with Jenny also. Same thing again photos been taken away from our account

We had so many Facebook accounts open.

Jenny phoned in two sandra ask lee stop phoning me I never left my phone on table main room net fix since we got married Jenny cousin never been kner since got married almost three years Jenny had phone call saying this is emma keep away from sandra and lee has what Jenny said two Sandra

AFTER that we still rowing like mad all this is that some 1 pretending two be me

RESAN BEING WHY Open another Facebook account AFTER WE GOT MARRIED.

Open another face book account: on my 50th birthday September 17th another girl came in that I been caused of NAME BY Jorde.

Me and my wife still at same church Swansea. Long time 3 days per week praying on Thursday also round world two.

Anyway I been blamed seeing jorde two. That person pretending be me on face again ain't nice. On same day there was a skip in our church park saying when is

the divorce lee Sandra WHAT HAPPENED 3 of us drove in to the car park Thursday me wife dave.

Dave went by the skip while paul Out side by skip me and wife inside church praying. Dave came in two me lee have something show u ok dave I come out dave said important lee. Went out my self saw word divorce when lee sandra Thursday after wards. On a peace of plastics. Some 1 even said le.

Having child with jorde on face book two been having this message for long time. Facebook problems also then on messenger chat maps was showing up that's strange after my wife showed realy mad.

HOW COULD THAT BE DONE to us On social networking Media

FACEBOOK HACKED Every time we been parking Our car up.

Different carpark I had photo done while walking two get our car then photo been taken of me long side our church posted in about me and jorde having child never happened.

All JEALOUS OF ME. Person pretending to be all. Wife have daughter named cody.

By cody

Cody my step daughter all In the past we all had photos done.

Me wife cody out front garden hard photo done. Word been said that on the Image saying photo u dirty bastard image photo two.

Sandra wife have son name kurt on face book. Time been going well two at time.

Me and kurt last minit had chat on messenger. Step son I don't have children I been blamed two while talking two kurt on messenger.

Saying on text while phone chat messanger. Words came in as saying word text then person. Pretending that words were said

On mobile messenger. At the time we bring this virus two u ain't happy that 1.

Then more went on. Cant believe this.

Again another face book open up again. Been thret two by local people pretending two be me had phone calls

wanted come best me up two while we on lock down.

I'm not very happy at all Of this person pretending to be me.

GOOGLE

I phoned them free UK number.

I ask google team what I do about face
told me phone net work provider up
explain that I have been spoofing on net.

BT AFTER EE

I phoned bt up and ask them. What can
I do about this. They told me phone law
up. So I did law want do anything about
face book.

Phoned net work up they ask me.

Join up with pc curry team know how
joined up with them control assistant in
side program Basied uk wide

Facebook

Open another account up. Same thing again different women. Name by sarah and ASHLEY. Also had started again. Been having phone calls coming in two. Photo image taken off me long side our church.

MAPS

Been posted two chat list. What could be done. Only report as u see them.

Trust friend

Most days u only can talk two trust friends about ur account.

This morning news I even phoned them up explaind about account sorry cant do nothing. This been going on good while I said phone police that's all I can do phone them back up.

Jeremy Kyle

At the time of their show was on I phoned them up said to me that messing my mind up.

What can do about this. Even my wife keeps an eye. On me two while having fag out back. Also thinking that I been seeing sertin girl.

We kept rowing for nothing. Now that herd as u see at the time.

Facebook hacked

Twitter Instagram

My Idea that face book should have control centre. Open so that all accounts can be safe and secure. I also done full check trying two Solf our problems out About face book two.

AVG

I have phoned them up in the past two had them in side our computer they wanted £2000

At

Another scam. I really been reading about Is AVG also Malware. 67%fall out of 100%.

Be careful full what u all doing with photos on your device. Keep them safe two 1 side. If u cant close accounts. Down at all they have fake ur account at all times.

thank for reading.

Take care be safe on net

Even rich or poor

From mr lee waite

This is part 2

- 35 -

Joshua

For colour

I remember when I was young child. Name film came out.

Joshua, like came of chess with me. Remember that film all As we all round world this is seriously what is happening on Social media services net.

IP address can be hacked in through IP ADDRESS with out any 1 knows. The service what happens About Being hacked on net work.

When u open gmail account open up all safe a ok until the thing is when we

all join up on Facebook cause of IP addresses can be found on net codes I come up better idea that no body want get hacked any more Through Facebook.

I only can explain

Two Facebook what can be done not two be hacked anymore also report easy and call centres reopen up.

This will be good opportunity two Facebook for whole world be safe and well for us all really like two meet up with face book community team.

All so go on news Video life

Thank you looking at part 2 colour really look for ear from you our world so seriously about being hacked internet.

Scammer

Need this change round bit world wide be safe on international community social media services uk and alive world.

We all over world need to be very safe and secure security services code protected all over world once can thank u mr lee waite.

It's all corrupted data bases issues problems.

DATE 14/07/2020

Person still pretending. Still using account again through Google gmail.

Some 1 using my name while that person having affair using our name.

www.ingramcontent.com/pod-product-compliance
Lightning Source LLC
Chambersburg PA
CBHW051423250726
48655CB00003B/1200